I0818557

UNBREAKABLE SPORTS RECORDS?

BASKETBALL RECORDS

THAT WILL BE TOUGH TO BEAT

Patrick Donnelly

Mitchell Lane
PUBLISHERS

Mitchell Lane
PUBLISHERS

mitchelllanepub.com

2001 SW 31st Avenue
Hallandale, FL 33009

First Edition, 2026.
Author: Patrick Donnelly
Designer: Ed Morgan
Editor: Tammy Gagne

Series: Unbreakable Sports Records?
Title: Basketball Records That Will Be Tough to Beat

Library bound ISBN: 979-8-89260-723-0
eBook ISBN: 979-8-89260-732-2

Photo credits: cover, p. 7, 13, 17, 19, 23, 25, 27, 31, 33, 35, 37, 39, 43, 45, 47, 51, 53, 55, 56 Alamy; p. 11, 15 freepik.com

CONTENTS

INTRODUCTION

The CLOSEST ANYONE HAD COME

Kobe Bryant was on fire. The Los Angeles Lakers guard was lighting up the scoreboard against the Toronto Raptors on January 22, 2006. Bryant had 26 points at halftime, and he was just getting started.

The Lakers trailed by 18 in the third quarter when Bryant went to work. He made nearly every shot he attempted. He scored on drives to the basket. He hit pull-up jump shots. He drained long three-pointers. He made 18 free throws on 20 attempts. The Lakers were in the lead by the end of the third quarter, but Bryant still wasn't finished.

INTRODUCTION

The crowd at the Staples Center buzzed as the Lakers' star player kept racking up points. Fans counted them out loud as they rallied behind Bryant, wondering how high his total would go. By the time the Lakers won the game, 122–104, he had taken nearly half the team's total shots. He was already seen as one of the best players in Lakers' history, and he was cementing that image with this incredible performance.

Bryant finished the game with 81 points. This total broke the Lakers' single-game record by 10 points. It was also the most points any player in the National Basketball Association (NBA) had scored in one game in almost forty-four years. Yet Bryant still wasn't close to breaking the league's record for the most points scored in a game.

Some records seem like they'll never be topped—until someone breaks them, that is. These five players set the bar high with their amazing achievements. Time will tell, however, whether their records are truly unbreakable.

THE CLOSEST ANYONE HAD COME

Kobe Bryant challenged the single-game scoring record in January 2006.

CHAPTER ONE

WILT CHAMBERLAIN'S 100-POINT GAME

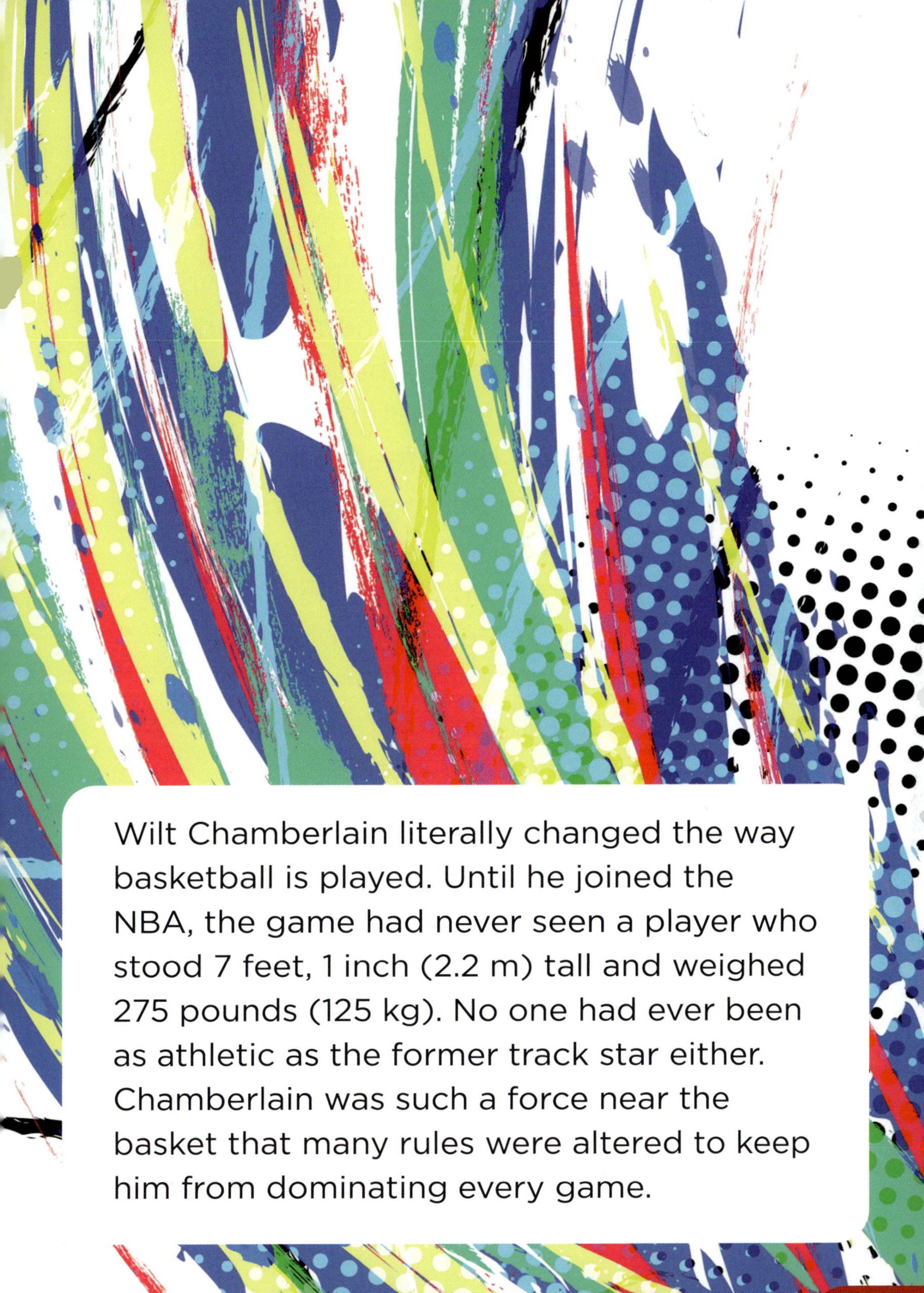

Wilt Chamberlain literally changed the way basketball is played. Until he joined the NBA, the game had never seen a player who stood 7 feet, 1 inch (2.2 m) tall and weighed 275 pounds (125 kg). No one had ever been as athletic as the former track star either. Chamberlain was such a force near the basket that many rules were altered to keep him from dominating every game.

Take, for instance, the area between the free throw line and the basket, otherwise known as the lane. When Chamberlain entered the NBA in 1959, the lane was 12 feet (3.7 m) wide. Five years later, the league expanded the lane to 16 feet (4.9 m) wide. That helped give defensive players a better chance at rebounding missed shots. Offensive players aren't allowed to stay in the lane as long as defensive players. Many other current rules reflect changes caused at least in part by Chamberlain, including **goaltending** and free throw shooting.

According to *Wilt: Larger Than Life,* a biography of Chamberlain, his longtime teammate Jerry West said, "There is no doubt that Wilt was one of the greatest players ever to play the game of basketball. He was the only player the rules of the game were changed for. His dominance of his sport was overwhelming."

three-point circle
16 ft
free throw line
lane
basket

Chamberlain's dominance was never clearer than on March 2, 1962. He was twenty-five years old and in his third season as a center for the Philadelphia Warriors. The team was about to move to San Francisco because ownership felt it lacked support from the local fans. The Warriors moved a few of their home games to other cities in Pennsylvania. On Chamberlain's big night, the Warriors were hosting the New York Knicks in the city of Hershey.

The Knicks would finish the season with the worst record in the NBA's Eastern Division. And on that night in Hershey, starting center Phil Jordon was sidelined with the flu. This made New York the right opponent at the right time for Chamberlain to flex his muscles.

Wilt Chamberlain dominated the NBA with his size, strength, and quickness.

It might seem hard to believe today, but in the early 1960s, many NBA games weren't televised. For this reason, no video exists of Chamberlain's big night in Hershey. But the written details paint the picture of a man playing against boys. Chamberlain scored 23 points in the first quarter. He added 18 in the second quarter, and his 28 third-quarter points bumped him up to 69 heading into the game's final 12 minutes.

By this time, the crowd of more than 4,000 people at Hershey Sports Arena sensed they were witnessing history. They began chanting for the Warriors to "Give it to Wilt!" And as he continued to dominate the Knicks' backup centers, his point total continued to grow.

The Knicks didn't want to be on the wrong end of such a historic event. To prevent Chamberlain from scoring, they began fouling his teammates to prevent them from passing to their star center. No problem—the Warriors returned the favor, putting the Knicks on the free throw line immediately so they could get the ball back.

Finally, with 46 seconds left, Chamberlain hit a short jump shot to push his total to 100 points. It was the most points any NBA player had scored in a game. Fans stormed the court, and the officials called off the remainder of the game, giving the Warriors a 169–147 victory.

Elgin Baylor

Whose Record Did Chamberlain Beat?

Chamberlain broke his own record with this 100-point game. Two months earlier, he scored 78 points in a game, which was the most until his now-famous Hershey game. Before that, the record was held by Los Angeles Lakers forward Elgin Baylor. This future Hall of Famer scored 71 points against the New York Knicks at Madison Square Garden on November 15, 1960. Baylor didn't hold the record long, but over the next six decades, only Chamberlain and three other players scored more than 71 points in a game. Chamberlain did it five times.

"Wilt did this because he could," journalist Gary M. Pomerantz said in *The New York Times*. "He bent the sport to his will."

Chamberlain had plenty of other big games, as have other basketball stars. A player has scored at least 65 points in an NBA game twenty-seven times—Chamberlain was that player fifteen times. But he never scored more than 73 points in a game after his 100-point explosion. Some fans wonder what the difference was that night in Hershey. The answer may be found in the free throw totals. Chamberlain made just over 51 percent of his career free throws. But against the Knicks on that fateful night, he made 28 of 32 (87.5 percent) from the line.

Luka Dončić

Chasing Chamberlain's Record

Chamberlain's 100-point outburst might be basketball's safest record. The fact that nobody has come closer than Bryant's 81-point night shows how hard it will be to top. However, if any of today's current players has a chance, former Dallas Mavericks guard Luka Dončić might be the athlete. Dončić scored 73 points in a Mavericks victory over the Atlanta Hawks on January 26, 2024. Now a member of the Los Angeles Lakers, he's an explosive scorer who is equally comfortable shooting three-pointers and driving to the basket. And he hit 15 of 16 free throws against the Hawks, so fouling him isn't a great idea either.

CHAPTER TWO

Bill Russell's 11 NBA CHAMPIONSHIPS

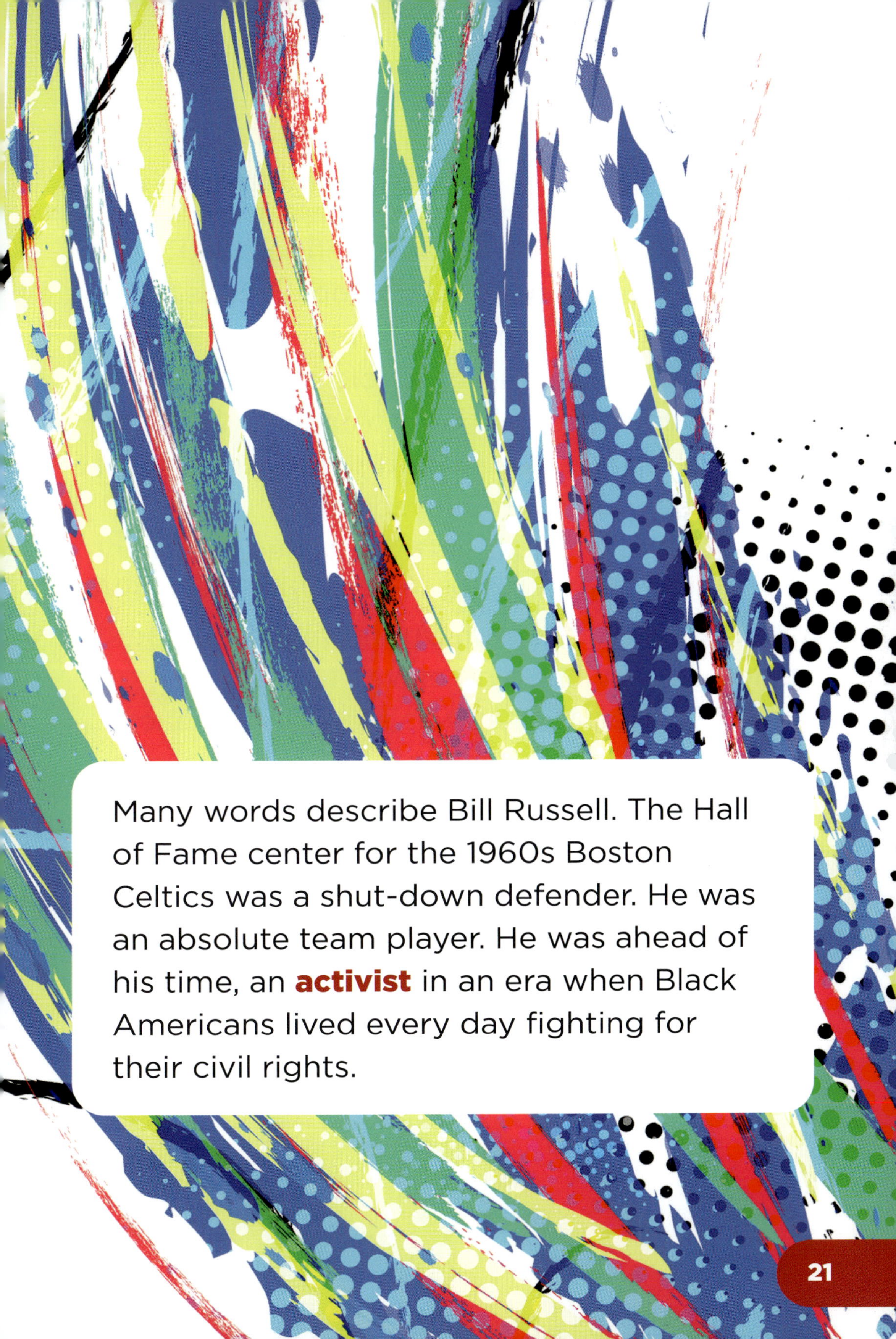

Many words describe Bill Russell. The Hall of Fame center for the 1960s Boston Celtics was a shut-down defender. He was an absolute team player. He was ahead of his time, an **activist** in an era when Black Americans lived every day fighting for their civil rights.

CHAPTER TWO

But the one word that best defines Bill Russell is winner. He won national championships at the University of San Francisco in 1955 and 1956. Then he led Team USA to a gold medal at the 1956 Olympics in Melbourne, Australia. He then joined the Celtics and helped them win their first NBA title during his rookie season.

But Russell was just getting started. He spent thirteen seasons in Boston before retiring in 1969 at the age of thirty-four. During that time, the Celtics won a whopping eleven NBA championships. Russell was a big part of each one. He was an All-Star in his last twelve seasons. A tireless defender, he averaged 42.3 minutes per game at center as he battled the league's other top players. He won the NBA Most Valuable Player (MVP) Award five times. And he even won his last two titles while serving as a player-coach after the Celtics hired him as the first Black head coach in NBA history.

George Mikan

Whose Record Did Russell Beat?

Before the Celtics started their epic run, no player had won more than five NBA titles. The league didn't begin until 1946, so there wasn't as much time to pile up the championships. The Minneapolis Lakers were the league's first **dynasty**. They won five titles between 1949 and 1954. Center George Mikan and power forward Jim Pollard played on all five championship teams. Point guard Slater Martin won four rings with those Lakers and a fifth with the St. Louis Hawks in 1958.

Russell was known for rising to the occasion when the spotlight was the brightest. Longtime *Boston Globe* columnist Bob Ryan pointed out that the Celtics player was undefeated in games in which his team's season was on the line. Ryan posted on Twitter, "Bill Russell 21–0 in winner-take-all games: All [National Collegiate Athletic Association] games, Olympic medal round, best-of-5s, best of 7s. Greatest résumé of anyone. Period."

Many NBA legends have important legacies. They include Magic Johnson and Larry Bird, who carried a friendly college rivalry over to the NBA and helped the league's popularity soar in the 1980s. Michael Jordan had a similar **impact** in the 1990s. But Russell's **legacy** is not to be overlooked. After all, only one uniform number has been retired throughout the NBA—Russell's number 6.

Bill Russell was a champion in college, the Olympics, and the NBA.

Writer Jack Hamilton said in *Slate* magazine, "Among basketball fans it's a frequent matter of debate as to when the 'modern NBA' starts: sometimes with the [American Basketball Association] **merger**, often with Johnson and Bird, occasionally with Jordan. But on its very best days, it starts with Bill Russell."

Anthony Edwards

Chasing Russell's Record

The landscape of the NBA has changed greatly since Russell and the Celtics dominated the league in the 1960s. Players now have much more freedom to change teams. That makes it harder to keep a team together long enough to challenge the 1960s Celtics for total championships. This might be the longest of all the longshots. For a player to win twelve NBA titles these days, he'd have to start young, stay healthy, and love the game enough to keep playing for years. Today, a few players fit that profile. Anthony Edwards of the Minnesota Timberwolves is one who might have the best chance.

CHAPTER THREE

Michael Jordan's 6 NBA Finals MVP AWARDS

Michael Jordan was already considered the greatest player of all time by many basketball fans. He didn't need to break new records to become a legend. But in Game 6 of the 1998 NBA Finals, that's just what he did.

Jordan's Chicago Bulls were in Utah, trying to close out the Jazz and win their sixth NBA title in eight years. Utah had the ball and a single-point lead with 36 seconds left to play. One more basket could help seal the win and force a deciding Game 7.

Instead, Jordan swooped in and stole the ball from future Hall of Famer Karl Malone. With 20 seconds left, the Bulls didn't call a timeout. They let Jordan do his thing. He dribbled across midcourt as the other nine players scrambled into position. Byron Russell, Utah's defensive wizard, lined up to guard Jordan near the top of the key. With 10 seconds left, Jordan made his move. He started toward the basket, which got Russell backpedaling. But instead of driving to the hoop, Jordan pulled up for an 18-foot (5.5-m) jump shot.

The ball swished through the net, giving the Bulls an 87–86 lead. The Jazz missed a final shot, and the Bulls were once again NBA champions.

Michael Jordan took his greatness to another level during the NBA playoffs.

It was a classic performance for Jordan. He finished the night with 45 points, four steals, and his sixth NBA Finals MVP Award. No player had ever been named the MVP of the Finals more than three times. And Jordan won those six awards in six Finals appearances. In other words, every time his Bulls reached the NBA Finals, Jordan rose to the occasion and was the best player in the series.

Jordan led the Bulls to three straight titles between 1991 and 1993. Then, after taking almost two years off to pursue a career in baseball, he came back to do it again, carrying the Bulls to three more titles between 1996 and 1998. Along the way, he conquered some of the game's all-time greats. They included Johnson's Lakers, Charles Barkley and the Suns, Shaquille O'Neal and the Magic, and finally the Jazz twice, denying Malone and John Stockton a chance at a title of their own.

Magic Johnson

Whose Record Did Jordan Beat?

Before Jordan started his run, Magic Johnson held the record for the most NBA Finals MVP Awards with three. Since Jordan's sixth award, only LeBron James has come close to challenging the record. The longtime star of the Cleveland Cavaliers, Miami Heat, and Los Angeles Lakers has won the NBA Finals MVP Award four times. He won it back-to-back with Miami in 2012 and 2013. James returned to Cleveland and was named Finals MVP in 2016. And he brought home the award with the Lakers in 2020.

According to *The New York Times*, Jordan's former teammate Charles Oakley once said, "A lot of teams probably could've won a ring if Michael Jordan wasn't in the NBA. But he was there, and you had to go through him, and it wasn't easy."

While his last Finals game was amazing, it wasn't Jordan's only jaw-dropping moment on the game's biggest stage. He scored 38 points when he was racked with flu symptoms in Game 5 of the 1997 NBA Finals. He dropped 55 points on Phoenix in Game 4 of the 1993 Finals. And he buried the Portland Trail Blazers with 46 points in Game 5 of the 1992 Finals. Along the way, he also turned himself into the best two-way player in the league.

Michael Jordan celebrates another big moment in the NBA Finals.

"People told him . . . he wasn't really a good defensive player," Bulls head coach Phil Jackson said in the documentary *Michael Jordan to the Max*. "And he found a way not only to become a great defensive player, but the best defensive player in the NBA. This guy said, 'Those are my weaknesses. I'm gonna figure out how to make those my strengths.' And he did it."

In six NBA Finals, Jordan played 35 games and averaged 33.6 points, 6.0 rebounds, and 6.0 assists. It's no wonder he's considered by many the NBA's greatest of all time.

Bulls head coach Phil Jackson discusses strategy with Jordan.

CHAPTER THREE

Shai Gilgeous-Alexander

Chasing Jordan's Record

It's hard to predict who might beat Jordan's amazing record. The best candidate would have to be talented enough to be dominant and young enough to maximize his chances. He'd also have to play for a team that has the depth and commitment to play in multiple NBA Finals. Shai Gilgeous-Alexander of the Oklahoma City Thunder checks enough of those boxes to be a possible contender.

CHAPTER FOUR

Hakeem Olajuwon's 3,830 CAREER BLOCKS

Few plays in sports are more discouraging than a big blocked shot. A player drives the lane, looking to make a layup or a short jumper. Then along comes a giant hand to swat the ball into the third row of the stands—or back in the shooter's face. A big blocked shot can change a game. It fires up the crowd, intimidates the opponents, and can even fuel a big comeback.

Nobody did it better than Hakeem Olajuwon. He played in eighteen NBA seasons—seventeen with the Houston Rockets, and one with the Toronto Raptors. Through his career, the 7-foot (2.1-m) Olajuwon used his size, speed, and agility to block a record 3,830 shots.

CHAPTER FOUR

Olajuwon grew up in Nigeria, where he played soccer long before he picked up a basketball. He played goalkeeper, using his long arms and big hands to swat away balls and deny his opponents' scoring opportunities. When Olajuwon was seventeen, a friend asked him to join the school basketball team for a tournament, and he fell in love with the sport.

He received a basketball scholarship from the University of Houston, where he quickly became a dominant force on defense. The Houston Rockets made Olajuwon the first pick of the 1984 NBA Draft. He teamed with Ralph Sampson, who was 7 feet, 4 inches (2.2 m) tall, to form Houston's "Twin Towers."

Kareem Abdul-Jabbar

Whose Record Did Olajuwon Beat?

Respect must be paid to Hall of Fame center Kareem Abdul-Jabbar. In his twenty-year NBA career with the Bucks and the Lakers, Abdul-Jabbar was credited with 3,189 blocks. However, when Abdul-Jabbar began his career with the Milwaukee Bucks in 1969, the NBA didn't track blocked shots. The block didn't become an official part of basketball **statistics** until 1973. This means that four seasons' worth of Abdul-Jabar's blocked shots weren't counted. He averaged 2.6 blocks per game in his career, and he played 321 games in his first four seasons. This could mean that he had another 834 blocks, which would put him back atop the career list.

Jim Petersen joined the Rockets in the same draft. He was Olajuwon's longtime backup and practice partner, getting an up-close view of the Hall of Famer's greatness. "He was unbelievable, just physically the way he was put together," Petersen told *The Athletic*. "He was so strong, and he was so quick and agile. The league had never seen a player like him before." Peterson described Olajuwon as strong and fast with quick hands—"the way that he could just elevate and jump off."

When he entered the NBA, Olajuwon was still perfecting his offensive game. But he was already elite at the other end of the court. He finished second in the league with 220 blocks as a rookie. That was the first of twelve straight seasons in which Olajuwon finished in the NBA's top five in the category. He blocked at least 10 shots in 12 games, achieving his personal best of 12 blocks twice.

HAKEEM OLAJUWON'S 3,830 CAREER BLOCKS

Hakeem Olajuwon shoots over the Celtics' Robert Parish.

He also was one of the first foreign-born players to make his mark in the world's top basketball league. Today's NBA is a melting pot of nationalities, thanks to the sport's growth overseas. Fellow Hall of Famer and shot-blocking legend Dikembe Mutombo said those players owe Olajuwon thanks for paving the path for them.

"Hakeem is my idol," Mutombo said in *The Athletic*. "He inspired all of us. I think if Hakeem hadn't done it the way he did it, not many people would've followed. He opened that door. I talk about him being the king of Africa. He opened that door for us. He sat on that throne so we can follow."

Victor Wembanyama

Chasing Olajuwon's Record

San Antonio Spurs center Victor Wembanyama is the ideal candidate to take down Olajuwon's record. The 7-foot-4-inch (2.2-m) forward joined the Spurs from his native France as a nineteen-year-old in 2023. As a rookie, he blocked 254 shots. That's more than any other NBA player had blocked in a season since 2016. Wembanyama isn't just tall. He's athletic, a leaper who can swoop in from any angle to redirect a shot. If he continues on this track, he'll be a menace for his opponents for years to come.

CHAPTER FIVE

LeBron James's 40,490 (and Counting) CAREER POINTS

On an ordinary Tuesday night in February 2023, LeBron James turned a Lakers-Thunder game into one for the history books. In the third quarter of an eventual 133–130 victory for Oklahoma City, James made a shot few in attendance will ever forget.

CHAPTER FIVE

He had the ball near the top of the key. The rest of the Lakers cleared out, allowing him to go one-on-one with Thunder forward Kenrich Williams. James took three dribbles, eventually pulling up for a fadeaway jumper at the free throw line.

As the ball swished through the net, the hometown crowd exploded in cheers. James ran down to the other end of the court, arms raised. It was a simple 14-foot (4.3-m) shot, but it was also much more than that. The basket gave James 38,388 career points. That's more than any player had scored in NBA history.

Kareem Abdul-Jabbar

Whose Record Did James Beat?

Kareem Abdul-Jabbar wasn't just a shot-blocking standout. He could also put the ball in the hoop. Abdul-Jabbar scored 38,387 points in twenty NBA seasons. He broke Wilt Chamberlain's career scoring record in the 1983–84 season, then spent another five seasons adding to his totals. His record lasted almost forty years before James passed Abdul-Jabbar in 2022.

CHAPTER FIVE

James arrived in the NBA as an eighteen-year-old with more **hype** than any rookie in recent memory. He'd been featured on the cover of *Sports Illustrated* when he was still in high school. His hometown Cleveland Cavaliers made him the first overall pick in the 2003 NBA Draft. And against all odds, his performance **surpassed** expectations.

On the way to winning the NBA Rookie of the Year Award, James averaged 20.9 points per game—as a *teenager*. And twenty-one years later, that scoring average remained the lowest of his career. The four-time NBA MVP only won one scoring title, when he averaged 30.0 points per game in the 2007–08 season. But he became one of the most consistent scorers in NBA history. Standing a burly 6 feet, 9 inches (1.2 m) tall, James can look a bit like a runaway semitruck as he barrels toward the basket. But he also has a silky touch from the outside, with three-pointers becoming a bigger part of his **arsenal** as he has grown older.

LeBron James faced huge expectations when he began his NBA career at age nineteen.

CHAPTER FIVE

As longtime NBA writer Leigh Montville noted in *Forbes*, "LeBron's **efficiency** and dominance cannot be swept under the rug. His 'bully ball' style on offense proves to be unstoppable."

But James is much more than just a scorer. He led the league in assists in the 2019–20 season, has averaged more than 7.0 rebounds per game in his career, and twice finished second in Defensive Player of the Year voting.

Tyronn Lue was James's head coach in Cleveland when the Cavaliers won the NBA title in 2016. Lue told *The Athletic* that James was an unlikely candidate to break the all-time scoring record, because his focus was on more than just putting the ball in the hoop. "The guy was a pass-first guy, a guy who always wants to get teammates involved, make your teammates look good, get every coach he's ever played with, get them paid," said Lue. "And then, turn around and look up and he's about to be the all-time leading scorer in NBA history? Yeah."

James is comfortable driving through traffic to score or sinking long jump shots over the defense.

CHAPTER FIVE

Kevin Durant

Chasing James's Record

Kevin Durant began the 2024–25 season second among active players with 28,924 career points. The only person with more points was James. At age thirty-five, Durant was an **elite** shooter, but he also uses his 6-foot-11-inch (2.1-m) frame to score inside. With a career average of 27.3 points per game, Durant ranks among the NBA's top 10 all-time scorers. Depending on how high James sets the bar, Durant has a chance to steal the NBA career scoring crown before he retires.

Think FAST!

Test your new knowledge of basketball by answering the following questions.

1. **Why did officials stop the game when Wilt Chamberlain scored his 100th point?**
   A. The Knicks wanted to quit.
   B. The ball was stolen.
   C. Fans stormed the court.
   D. The lights went out.

2. **How many NBA titles did Bill Russell win?**
   A. 13
   B. 3
   C. 11
   D. 9

3. **From whom did Michael Jordan steal the ball at the end of Game 6 of the 1998 NBA Finals?**
   A. John Stockton
   B. Charles Barkley
   C. Magic Johnson
   D. Karl Malone

4. **What was the highest number of shots Olajuwon blocked in one game?**
   A. 17
   B. 12
   C. 13
   D. 10

5. **Who were the Lakers playing when LeBron James broke the NBA career scoring record?**
   A. Cleveland Cavaliers
   B. Houston Rockets
   C. Oklahoma City Thunder
   D. San Antonio Spurs

Answers: 1. C 2. C 3. D 4. B 5. C

Glossary

activist
Someone who takes part in protests to bring about political or social change

arsenal
A collection of skills an athlete can use in competition

dynasty
A team or other group with a long history of success

efficiency
Effective use of time and energy

elite
Superior in skills and ability

goaltending
A basketball violation in which a player interferes with a shot when it is on its downward arc or is on or over the rim

hype
Frequent and excessively positive media attention

impact
A strong effect on someone or something

legacy
An impact left behind by a player

merger
A joining of two organizations when one absorbs the other

statistics
A collection of data

surpassed
Exceeded

Find Out More

IN PRINT

Donnelly, Patrick. *Football Records That Will Be Tough to Beat*. Mitchell Lane Publishing, 2026.

Flynn, Brendan. *NBA Encyclopedia for Kids*. Abdo Publishing, 2022.

Mann, Dionna L. *LeBron James vs. Michael Jordan: Basketball Legends Face Off*. Capstone Press, 2025.

ON THE INTERNET

***Basketball Reference*, n.d.**
www.basketball-reference.com.

***Naismith Memorial Basketball Hall of Fame*, n.d.**
www.hoophall.com.

***NBA*, n.d.**
www.nba.com.

Index

About the Author

Patrick Donnelly is a sportswriter and author who lives in Minneapolis, Minnesota. He's written more than 100 books about sports, many of them about basketball. He frequently covers the Minnesota Timberwolves for the Associated Press. He's still bummed that the Lakers moved to Los Angeles in 1960, even though he wasn't alive yet.